Belongs to

Letters to my Grandchild

5-18-19

12

Who would think there could be magic in this simple number. Your mom + dad have waited a long time to hit this number. The First Trimester! So much anxiety, concern, tears + fears --- and then JOY!

Your mom + I share something so important — the ~~innte~~ innate desire to be a mom

+ today I am lucky enough to be there when we find out if you will be my granddaughter or grandson

Letters to my Grandchild

Letters to my Grandchild

....

....

....

....

....

....

....

....

....

....

....

....

....

....

....

....

....

....

....

....

....

....

....

....

....

....

....

....

Letters to my Grandchild

Letters to my Grandchild

Letters to my Grandchild

Letters to my Grandchild

Letters to my Grandchild

Letters to my Grandchild

Letters to my Grandchild

Letters to my Grandchild

Letters to my Grandchild

Letters to my Grandchild

Letters to my Grandchild

Letters to my Grandchild

Letters to my Grandchild

Letters to my Grandchild

Letters to my Grandchild

Letters to my Grandchild

Letters to my Grandchild

Letters to my Grandchild

Letters to my Grandchild

Letters to my Grandchild

Letters to my Grandchild

Letters to my Grandchild

Letters to my Grandchild

Letters to my Grandchild

Letters to my Grandchild

Letters to my Grandchild

Letters to my Grandchild

Letters to my Grandchild

Letters to my Grandchild

Letters to my Grandchild

Letters to my Grandchild

Letters to my Grandchild

Letters to my Grandchild

Letters to my Grandchild

Letters to my Grandchild

Letters to my Grandchild

Letters to my Grandchild

Letters to my Grandchild

Letters to my Grandchild

Letters to my Grandchild

Letters to my Grandchild

Letters to my Grandchild

Letters to my Grandchild

Letters to my Grandchild

Letters to my Grandchild

Letters to my Grandchild

Letters to my Grandchild

Letters to my Grandchild

Letters to my Grandchild

Letters to my Grandchild

Letters to my Grandchild

Letters to my Grandchild

Letters to my Grandchild

Letters to my Grandchild

Letters to my Grandchild

Letters to my Grandchild

Letters to my Grandchild

Letters to my Grandchild

Letters to my Grandchild

Letters to my Grandchild

Letters to my Grandchild

Letters to my Grandchild

Letters to my Grandchild

Letters to my Grandchild

Letters to my Grandchild

Letters to my Grandchild

Letters to my Grandchild

Letters to my Grandchild

Letters to my Grandchild

Letters to my Grandchild

Letters to my Grandchild

Letters to my Grandchild

Letters to my Grandchild

Letters to my Grandchild

Letters to my Grandchild

Letters to my Grandchild

Letters to my Grandchild

Letters to my Grandchild

Letters to my Grandchild

Letters to my Grandchild

Letters to my Grandchild

Letters to my Grandchild

Letters to my Grandchild

Letters to my Grandchild

Letters to my Grandchild

Letters to my Grandchild

Letters to my Grandchild

Letters to my Grandchild

Letters to my Grandchild

Letters to my Grandchild

Letters to my Grandchild

Letters to my Grandchild

Letters to my Grandchild

Letters to my Grandchild

Letters to my Grandchild

Letters to my Grandchild

Letters to my Grandchild

Letters to my Grandchild

Letters to my Grandchild

Letters to my Grandchild

Letters to my Grandchild

Letters to my Grandchild

Letters to my Grandchild

Letters to my Grandchild

Letters to my Grandchild

Letters to my Grandchild

Letters to my Grandchild

Letters to my Grandchild

Letters to my Grandchild

Letters to my Grandchild

Letters to my Grandchild

Letters to my Grandchild

Letters to my Grandchild

Letters to my Grandchild

Letters to my Grandchild

Letters to my Grandchild

Letters to my Grandchild

Letters to my Grandchild

....

....

....

....

....

....

....

....

....

....

....

....

....

....

....

....

....

....

....

....

....

....

....

....

....

....

....

....

Letters to my Grandchild

Letters to my Grandchild

Letters to my Grandchild

Letters to my Grandchild

Letters to my Grandchild